A Kid's Guide to Understanding Parents

A Children's Book about Parent-Child Relationships

by

Joy Wilt

Illustrated by Ernie Hergenroeder

Educational Products Division
Word, Incorporated
Waco, Texas

Author

JOY WILT is creator and director of Children's Ministries, an organization that provides resources "for people who care about children"—speakers, workshops, demonstrations, consulting services, and training institutes. A certified elementary school teacher, administrator, and early childhood specialist, Joy is also consultant to and professor in the master's degree program in children's ministries for Fuller Theological Seminary. Joy is a graduate of LaVerne College, LaVerne, California (B.A. in Biological Science), and Pacific Oaks College, Pasadena, California (M.A. in Human Development). She is author of three books, *Happily Ever After, An Uncomplicated Guide to Becoming a Superparent,* and *Taming the Big Bad Wolves,* as well as the popular *Can-Make-And-Do Books.* Joy's commitment "never to forget what it feels like to be a child" permeates the many innovative programs she has developed and her work as lecturer, consultant, writer, and—not least—mother of two children, Christopher and Lisa.

Artist

ERNIE HERGENROEDER is founder and owner of Hergie & Associates (a visual communications studio and advertising agency). With the establishment of this company in 1975, "Hergie" and his wife, Faith, settled in San Jose with their four children, Lynn, Kathy, Stephen, and Beth. Active in community and church affairs, Hergie is involved in presenting creative workshops for teachers, ministers, and others who wish to understand the techniques of communicating visually. He also lectures in high schools to encourage young artists toward a career in commercial art. Hergie serves as a consultant to organizations such as the Police Athletic League (PAL), Girl Scouts, and religious and secular corporations. His ultimate goal is to touch the hearts of kids (8 to 80) all over the world—visually!

ISBN: 0-8499-8132-8
Library of Congress Catalog Card Number: 79-53569

Joseph Paul, Editor

The educational concepts presented in the Ready-Set-Grow book series are also featured in a music songbook and longplay record. For further information concerning these materials see your local bookstore or write Word, Incorporated, 4800 West Waco Drive, Waco, Texas 76710.

Contents

Introduction

A Kid's Guide to Understanding Parents is one of a series of books. The complete set is called *Ready-Set Grow!*

A Kid's Guide to Understanding Parents is specifically designed so that children can either read the book themselves or have it read to them. This can be done at home, church, or school. When reading to children, it is not necessary to complete the book at one sitting. Concern should be given to the attention span of the individual child and his or her comprehension of the subject matter.

A Kid's Guide to Understanding Parents is designed to involve the child in the concepts that are being taught. This is done by simply and carefully explaining each concept and then asking questions that invite a response from the child. It is hoped that by answering the questions the child will personalize the concept and, thus, integrate it into his or her thinking.

There are many different kinds of parents. There are biological parents, adopted parents, stepparents, and foster parents. But no matter what kind of parents a child has, he or she needs to be able to deal with them in a constructive way.

A Kid's Guide to Understanding Parents shows children that their parents are people just like they are. Both share a lot in common. They experience many of the same bodily functions, many of the same feelings and needs, and, like children, are not perfect.

Parents also care and are often responsible for their children. Because of this, children need to understand the things parents do. So, A Kid's Guide to Understanding Parents carefully explains that parents establish and enforce rules, and educate and encourage their children.

Most of the time parents do these things for the right reasons and in the right way. But, because parents are not perfect, they sometimes are unfair and unkind. A Kid's Guide to Understanding Parents gives children constructive advice on what to do when this happens and how to establish a good relationship with their parents. Children who grow up understanding these concepts will be better equipped to live healthy, productive lives.

A Kid's Guide to Understanding Parents

If you are a child, you probably live with one or two adults who take care of you and are responsible for you. These adults are probably your parents.

There are many kinds of parents. One kind is "biological parents."
Biological parents are also called "natural parents" or "birth parents."

When sperm from a man's body gets together with an egg in a woman's
body, the woman becomes pregnant. About nine months after a woman
becomes pregnant, she gives birth to a child. The man whose sperm
fertilized the egg and the woman who gave birth to the child are the
child's biological parents.

A child does not always live with his or her biological parents. Sometimes the biological parents die or can't raise their child.

When either of these things happens, the child might be adopted by one or two other adults. When an adult adopts a child, he or she promises to take care of and be responsible for the child until the child grows up and can take care of himself or herself.

An adult who adopts a child is called an "adopted parent."

Not all children live with biological or adopted parents. Sometimes when a child is being raised by two parents, one of the parents dies. If the parent who is still alive marries someone else, that person becomes the child's "stepparent."

Sometimes a child's parents get a divorce. If either parent marries someone else, that person becomes the child's "stepparent."

Sometimes a child does not live with a biological, adopted, or stepparent.

There are several reasons for this. One reason is that the child's parents have died, and it has not been decided who the child's new parents will be.

A second reason is that the child's parents have gotten a divorce, and it has not been decided which parent the child will live with.

A third reason is that it has been decided that the child needs to spend some time away from his parents.

When any of these things happens to a child, he or she goes to live with one or two adults called "foster parents." Usually the child stays with them until things are worked out for him or her.

AND THERE'S WONDERFUL CECILE!
WE'RE LUCKY THAT YOU CAME TO LIVE WITH US WHILE THINGS WERE GETTING STRAIGHTENED OUT FOR YOU AT HOME.
FAMILY ALBUM
LETS GET A PICTURE OF CECILE FOR OUR FAMILY ALBUM.
OK! AND I WANT TO GET A PICTURE OF MOM AND DAD FOR ME TO KEEP FOREVER, BECAUSE THEY ARE THE BEST FOSTER PARENTS A KID COULD EVER HAVE!

Who do you live with?

Do you live with a mother?   Yes_____   No_____

If you live with a mother, is she your:

biological parent_____

adopted parent_____

stepparent_____

foster parent_____

Do you live with a father?   Yes_____   No_____

If you live with a father, is he your:

                                                 biological parent_____

                                                 adopted parent_____

                                                 stepparent_____

                                                 foster parent_____

Do you have any other parents that you do not live with?
Which of the four kinds of parents are they?

No matter who your parents are, no matter which ones you live with, your parents are the most important people in your life. This is why you need to be able to deal with them in a healthy and constructive way.

To do this, there are several things you need to know and understand.

Chapter 1

Parents Are People

Like you, parents are people.

Because they are, both you and your parents experience a lot of the same things.

Parents experience a lot of the same bodily functions that you do.

Parents eat and sleep.

Some parents snore when they sleep.

Parents go to the bathroom. They sometimes throw up when they are sick.

Parents sneeze and cough, hiccup, burp, and pass gas. Sometimes their stomachs growl when they get hungry.

GROWL

Because parents are people, like you, they experience many of the same feelings that you do.

Parents experience anger. Sometimes they get very mad.

Parents experience guilt. Sometimes they feel as though they have done something wrong.

Parents experience jealousy. Sometimes they wish they were like another person or that they had something another person has.

Parents experience grief. Sometimes they feel sad.

BOB IS AWAY ON A BUSINESS
TRIP, ALL THE KIDS ARE AT
CAMP, ALL MY FRIENDS
ARE BUSY OR OUT OF
TOWN, AND I'M SO
LONELY I CAN'T
STAND IT!

Parents experience rejection. Sometimes they feel that they are unwanted.

Parents experience humilation. Sometimes they feel embarrassed or put down.

Parents experience frustration. Sometimes they feel uptight and discouraged.

Parents experience fear and anxiety. Sometimes they feel frightened or scared, and sometimes they feel worried, nervous, or upset.

Parents experience defeat. Sometimes they feel as though they have lost or failed.

Parents experience happiness.

MR. ADAMS, I'VE CHANGED MY MIND ABOUT YOU. THE MORE I THINK ABOUT YOU, THE MORE I THINK YOU'RE THE RIGHT PERSON FOR THE JOB. CAN YOU START WORK ON MONDAY?

SURE!

Because parents are people, like you, they have needs.

Parents have physical needs. They need air, food, water, exercise . . .

and rest.

Parents have emotional needs. Parents need to have other people love them. They need others to value and care for them. Parents also have a need to love others.

Parents need to have other people respect them. They need others to admire them and think good things about them. Parents also have a need to respect others.

41

Parents need to have other people trust them. They need to have others know that they are honest and fair. Parents also have a need to trust others.

Parents need to feel secure. They need to know what to expect from others.

Parents have creative needs. Parents need to be creative. They need to have opportunities to make things and do things that they have never done before.

Parents have intellectual needs. Parents need to have opportunities to think and learn. They need to be able to be curious, explore, and discover new things.

Parents have ambition needs. Parents need to have a purpose and meaning in life. They have a need to feel useful and important.

Parents have recreational needs. Parents have a need to have fun.
They have a need to do things that they enjoy doing.

Because parents are people, like you, they are not perfect.

Sometimes parents have accidents.

Sometimes parents make wrong choices.

Sometimes parents make mistakes.

Sometimes parents have problems.

51

So remember, like you, parents are people.   They share
a lot in common with you.

They experience a lot of the same bodily functions that you do.

They experience many of the same feelings that you do.

They have the same kind of needs that you do.

They are not perfect, so they have accidents, make wrong choices, make
mistakes, and have problems.

Chapter 2

Parents Care and Are Often Responsible for Their Children.

Most parents love their children very much. Because they do, they care and are often responsible for them.

What are some of the ways parents want to <u>care</u> for their children?

They want to keep their children safe.

PLEASE COME HOME BEFORE 5:30.
IT'S DANGEROUS FOR YOU TO RIDE
YOUR BIKES IN THE DARK.

They also want to keep their children well.

Most parents want to help their children grow physically.

YOU NEED TO EAT VEGETABLES IF YOU EXPECT YOUR BODY TO GROW.

They also want to help their children grow mentally.

Most parents want their children to do what they feel is the right thing.

They also want other people to like and accept their children.

Most parents want their children to be successful.

They also want their children to be happy.

Most parents want the best things for their children.

WE NEED A CAR THAT IS BIG ENOUGH TO SEAT OUR FOUR CHILDREN COMFORTABLY.

THE NEW LUX MOBILE

They also want the best situations for their children.

So, because most parents care about their children, they want them to:

stay safe and well,

grow physically and mentally,

do the right thing,

be liked and accepted by others,

be successful and happy, and

have what is best for them.

Besides caring for their children, parents are also often <u>responsible</u> for them.

If children hurt themselves, their parents are often responsible for seeing that they are taken care of properly.

If children hurt someone else, their parents are often responsible for seeing that the person who was hurt is taken care of properly.

If children damage something that belongs to another person, the parents are often responsible for getting the damaged thing repaired.

If children destroy something that belongs to another person, the parents are often responsible for replacing the thing that has been destroyed.

YOUR SON HIT A BASEBALL THROUGH MY WINDOW AND BROKE IT, AND I EXPECT YOU TO HAVE IT FIXED, BECAUSE YOU'RE RESPONSIBLE FOR WHAT YOUR SON DOES!

So, in addition to caring, parents are often responsible when their children:

hurt themselves,

hurt others,

damage other peoples' things, or

destroy other peoples' things.

Chapter 3

Understanding the Things Parents Do

Parents are people with emotions and needs. They care and are often responsible for their children. Because this is so, parents do certain things.

Establishing Rules

Most parents make sure that there are RULES for their children to follow. Rules are guidelines that tell you how to act and what to do.

BECAUSE WE CARE FOR YOU AND ARE OFTEN RESPONSIBLE FOR THE THINGS YOU DO, WE MUST MAKE SURE THAT THERE ARE RULES FOR YOU TO FOLLOW.

Most parents make sure that there are <u>rules about space.</u>

IT'S OK FOR YOU TO BE IN THE KITCHEN, FAMILY ROOM, OR BATHROOM—ANYTIME YOU WANT TO. BUT YOU MUST GET PERMISSION IF YOU WANT TO GO INTO EACH OTHERS BEDROOMS. ALSO YOU MAY NOT EAT FOOD WHERE THERE'S CARPET ON THE FLOOR.

Most parents make sure that there are <u>rules about time</u>.

Most parents make sure that there are <u>rules about possessions</u>.

IF YOU WANT TO USE SOMETHING
THAT BELONGS TO SOMEONE ELSE,
YOU MUST GET THEIR PERMISSION
BEFORE YOU USE IT.

Most parents make sure that there are <u>rules about work.</u>

CECILE, I WOULD LIKE YOU TO DO THE DISHES. JOSHUA, I WOULD LIKE YOU TO EMPTY THE TRASH. KATE, I WANT YOU TO VACUUM. AND JOSH, I WOULD LIKE FOR YOU TO CLEAN THE BATHROOM. I WOULD APPRECIATE IT IF YOU HAD THESE JOBS DONE BY NOON TODAY.

Most parents make sure that there are <u>rules about play.</u>

Most parents make sure that there are <u>rules about family habits and customs</u>.

I WOULD LIKE FOR THE FAMILY TO SPEND SUNDAY AFTERNOON TOGETHER — WITHOUT VISITORS.

Enforcing Rules

Most parents enforce the rules that have been made. This means that they make sure that the rules are respected and obeyed. One way parents enforce rules is by TALKING to their children.

Another way parents enforce rules is by **LETTING THEIR CHILDREN SUFFER THE CONSEQUENCES** of breaking the rules.

This means that the children have to go through whatever happens to them because of breaking the rule.

Another way parents enforce rules is by PUNISHING their children.

One kind of punishment is <u>isolation</u>. This means putting the child somewhere where he or she is alone.

A second kind of punishment is <u>deprivation</u>. This means taking something away from the child that he or she really likes.

A third kind of punishment is <u>inflicted punishment</u>. This means having the child experience some kind of physical discomfort like shaking or spanking.

Educating Children

Most parents try to teach their children the best ways to live healthy, productive lives. One way parents do this is by helping their children learn certain skills.

Skills are good ways of behaving that help you handle the many different situations you face in life.

Some skills most parents try to teach their children are called
PERSONAL SKILLS.

Personal skills can help you:

feel good about the person you are,

think and learn effectively, and

find ways to get your physical, mental,
and emotional needs met.

87

Other skills most parents try to teach their children are called SOCIAL SKILLS.

Social skills can help you:

treat others as you would like to be treated,

handle disagreements and conflicts constructively,

contribute in a healthy way to your family life, and

establish and maintain positive friendships.

SO, ALL OF US SHOULD TREAT EACH OTHER WITH KINDNESS AND RESPECT. THAT'S GOOD MANNERS. AND DO YOU REMEMBER THE SPECIAL RULE THAT ALL GOOD MANNERS COME FROM?

YES! IT'S CALLED THE GOLDEN RULE. IT SAYS,"DO UNTO OTHERS AS YOU WOULD HAVE THEM DO UNTO YOU."

THAT'S RIGHT.

In addition to personal and social skills, most parents try to teach their children COPING SKILLS.

Coping skills can help you:

make decisions and solve problems,

understand and deal with opinions and prejudice,

handle unpleasant situations and experiences, and

manage your time, money, and possessions wisely.

Encouraging Children

Most parents use encouragement to help their children practice the personal, social, and coping skills needed to live healthy, productive lives.

Encouragement can:

help you believe you are somebody special,

give you confidence to do the things you know you can do, and

make you want to continue to try to learn new skills.

One way parents encourage their children is by ACCEPTING THEM.
This means that they show the child love and caring.

Another way parents encourage their children is by AFFIRMING THEM. This means that they say positive, kind things to the child.

Another way parents encourage their children is by REWARDING THEM.
This means that they give them something special for behaving properly.

BECAUSE YOU HAVE BEEN SO GOOD
ABOUT NOT EATING TOO MUCH
CANDY, I'D LIKE TO TAKE YOU OUT
FOR A HAMBURGER.

So remember, like you, parents have emotions and needs. They care and are often responsible for their children. This is why they do things like:

establish rules,

enforce rules,

educate their children, and

encourage their children.

Most of the time parents do these things for the right reasons and in the right way. But remember, parents are people, and because they are, they are not perfect.

Sometimes, the things parents do are unfair and unkind. What you do when your parents are this way depends a lot on the relationship you have with them.

The next chapter will tell you how to develop a good relationship with your parents and what you should do when they are unfair or unkind.

Chapter 4

Handling Parents Wisely

In order to handle your parents wisely, you need to have a good relationship with them.

All good relationships begin with knowing and remembering that:

every human being is special,

every human being is important,

no one is perfect,

a person improves best when he or she is allowed to
learn and grow at his or her own speed, and

every person has something valuable to give other people.

Once you understand how <u>all</u> good relationships begin, there are ten things you can do that will help you in your <u>special</u> relationship with your parents.

1. <u>Accept your parents the way they are.</u> Don't force them to change or be different.

2. **<u>Appreciate your parents.</u>** Tell your parents how much you like them, and praise them whenever you can.

3. **<u>Encourage your parents.</u>** Tell your parents that they are doing OK, and give them courage, hope, and confidence to keep trying.

4. **Put yourself in your parents place.** Try to understand how your parents think and feel, and respect their thoughts and feelings.

5. <u>**Avoid nagging or arguing with your parents.**</u>

6. <u>Admit it when you do something wrong or make a mistake that</u> <u>affects your parents.</u> Also tell them that you are sorry, and ask them to forgive you.

7. **Try to make your parents feel better when they do something wrong or make a mistake.** Do your best to forgive them.

8. **<u>Do something special once in a while to show your parents you</u> <u>love them.</u>**

9. Help them establish the rules and enforce them.

10. Talk to them kindly, honestly, and accurately.

I DON'T THINK IT'S DANGEROUS TO PLAY IN THE DARK. COULD YOU EXPLAIN WHY YOU THINK IT IS?

So, in order for you to develop the special relationship you have with your parents, there are ten things you need to remember.

1. Accept your parents.

2. Appreciate your parents.

3. Encourage your parents.

4. Put yourself in your parents' place.

5. Avoid nagging or arguing.

6.   Admit it when you are wrong, and tell them that you are sorry.

7.   Try to make your parents feel better.

8.   Do something special.

9.   Help them establish the rules and enforce them.

10. Talk to them.

If you are able to do these things, your relationship with your parents will most likely develop into a good one.

But having a good relationship with your parents does not mean that they will never be unkind or unfair.

When you find that your parents are being unkind or unfair, there is an important thing you can do:

TALK TO THEM.

Tell your parents how you feel. Explain to them how you would have preferred for them to have handled you or the situation.

Sometimes your parents will understand what you are saying and will agree with you.

But sometimes they won't. When your parents do not understand or agree with you, there is nothing you can do. Because your parents are often responsible for you they "have the final say." So you must cooperate with them and do as they say.

However . . .

Don't ever give up. Everytime a situation comes up when you feel your parents are being unfair or unkind, talk to them.

If you have a good relationship with them and if your observations about them are true, chances are your parents will agree with you a lot of the time.

Conclusion

Because your parents are people, they experience a lot of the same bodily functions that you do.

They also experience many of the same feelings that you do.

Because your parents are people, they have a lot of the same needs you do.

Like you, they also are not perfect.

Most parents care for their children and want them to:

stay safe and well,

grow physically and mentally,

do the right thing,

be liked and accepted by others,

be successful and happy, and

have what is best for them.

In addition to caring, parents are often responsible when their children:

hurt themselves,

hurt others,

damage other peoples' things, or

destroy other peoples' things.

Because parents care and are often responsible for their children, they do things like:

establish rules,

enforce rules,

educate their children, and

encourage their children.

Yet, sometimes parents can be unfair or unkind. But if you have a good relationship with them, chances are your parents will be fair and kind most of the time.

So remember, parents are people, too. And even though they are not perfect . . .

Thanks to your parents, there is YOU!